For Andy,

Many thanks for all the encouragement, inspiration, and great art direction. Most of all thank you for your friendship. You're the best —

Joe Neil

September 3, 1998

NYC

STYLE ON HAND

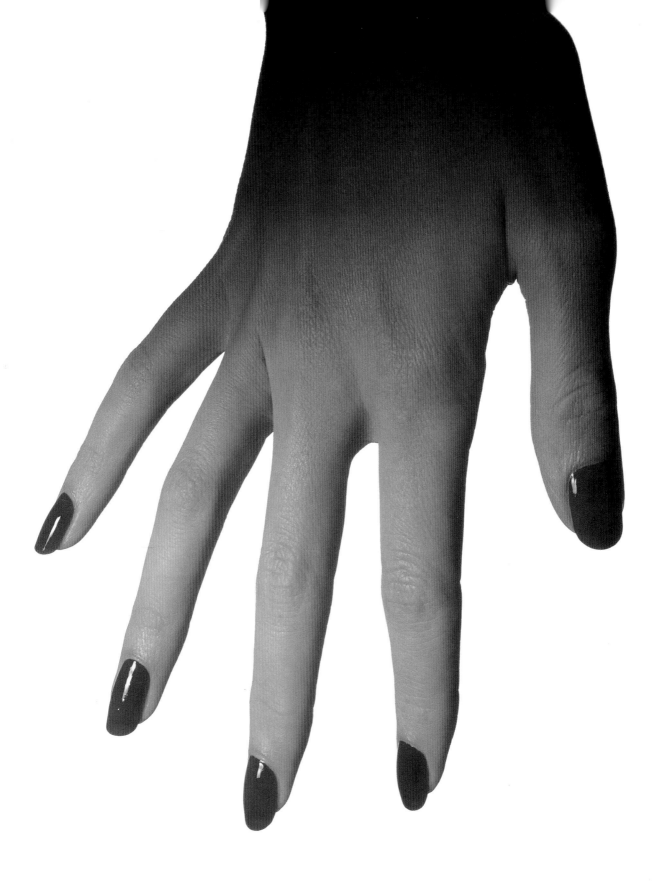

Perfect Nail and Skin Care

# STYLE ON HAND

BY ELISA FERRI AND LISA KENNY

WRITTEN WITH DANA EPSTEIN

PHOTOGRAPHY BY JOE NEIL

UNIVERSE

PREFACE BY STEPHANIE SEYMOUR

To my husband, Joel Bass, who put up with this whole ordeal
while we were getting married and on our honeymoon. The
love, support, and patience he provided exceeded all of my
dreams. I have the best one!
—Lisa Kenny-Bass

To my son, Frank Fimiano, in whose beautiful green
eyes I have always seen a reflection of the best self I could
ever hope to be. I live for your pride in me.
—Elisa Ferri

First published in the United States of America in 1998
by UNIVERSE PUBLISHING
A Division of Rizzoli International Publications, Inc.
300 Park Avenue South
New York, NY 10010

98 99 00 01 02/10 9 8 7 6 5 4 3 2 1

Library of Congress Catalog Card Number: 98-60897
Design and typography by Debra Drodvillo /notion/
Printed in England

# Contents

# Preface
### by Stephanie Seymour

The first thing I look at when I meet a person, besides, of course, their eyes, are their hands. No matter how pretty your hair is or how beautiful you look in that perfect little black dress, you cannot get around the fact that if your nails aren't done, *you're* not done.

When my hands and feet are well-groomed, I feel sexy, chic, and stylish. If I do not have time to go out and get a professional manicure and pedicure, I'll do my own mani and pedi using the great tips that Elisa has taught me. She has shown me that caring for your hands and feet doesn't have to be difficult. But once a month I love to treat myself to a pro—the hand and foot massage alone are worth it.

With *Style on Hand*, Elisa and Lisa provide the insider secrets that all women should know. Because when your hands look beautifully cared for, it gives you a feeling of confidence and style—and you never know when someone might reach to kiss your hand.

# Introduction

From the supermodel to the career woman to the teenager—today, everyone is excited about the myriad nail style possibilities. Granted, not everyone is born with a perfect set of nails. Therefore they need to be properly cared for, maintained, and—especially—nurtured. Just like a good haircut, healthy, glowing skin, and a fit body, well-groomed nails and hands are a fundamental part of looking and feeling your best. Today, nail care know-how is not only a beauty and grooming essential—it's a must.

In the nineties women have enjoyed exploring the endless variety of new nail styles. The unprecedented explosion of fresh new color possibilities as well as a riot of fun and exciting options—from conservative to daring to trendy—have made polishing nails a truly joyous event. In fact, most women today won't even leave the house without a finished manicure.

As we approach the new millennium, there is a growing trend toward perfecting at-home nail care. However, women often devote an inordinate amount of time to selecting the perfect nail color while letting hands fall victim of neglect. Well-moisturized, smooth skin and well-groomed cuticles provide the perfect canvas for a flawless manicure. Whatever your age—ten or one hundred—you will benefit from the invaluable information provided in this book.

Your favorite beauty supply stores offer all you need to get started for a lifetime of proper hand and nail care. Join us on a walk through the aisles. Pick up the essentials and get to work designing a nail care regimen to fit every lifestyle and occasion. We will apply these fundamental steps to creating a manageable foot-care routine as well.

Put the "Do Not Disturb" sign on the door so we can spend some quality time achieving a strong, stunning set of ten.

# Spa *and* rejuve

Today's beauty mantra indicates that looking good is all about feeling good. A well-balanced diet, physical fitness, smart skin care habits, and overall good health all play an integral role in how we look and how we feel. When we're happy, healthy, and calm, our skin is clear, our hair is shiny, and we look our best. Just as with skin and hair, healthy hands and nails start from within.

Based on the insights of several leading experts in the fields of nutrition, massage therapy, and dermatology, we have compiled the most up-to-date information for obtaining healthy hands and nails – from the inside-out.

*Eating a well-balanced, healthy diet of foods rich in vitamins is a sure way to achieve perfect nails and skin.*

*Our polish pick: two coats of grape creme.*

*Fruits, such as kiwi, are a good source of fiber, vitamin C, and beta carotene.*

*Eggs, along with milk,
cheeses, and yogurt,
are an excellent source
of calcium.*

*Grains, such as bread,
are packed full of iron.*

# Proper Nutrition:
## Food for Thought

### You Are What You Eat

Healthy-looking hands and nails are a direct result of proper nutrition. Skin
and nails are often the first places where vitamin, mineral, and protein deficiencies
can develop. Prime indicators of nutritional deficiencies are severely dry skin and
nails that are weak, fragile, and splitting. However, these symptoms can be helped
with vitamins A, B-complex, C, and E, as well as calcium, iron, zinc, and adequate
water intake (which is usually missing from our everyday diet).

### The Power of Protein

In order to build strong, healthy hands and nails, you will need to start with a diet
high in protein. Among its myriad benefits, protein provides us with the
natural building materials for new nails. Eating a diet high in protein will most
likely prevent those little white bands from appearing on the nail—a common
indication of a protein-deficient diet. Good sources of protein include meat, fish,
eggs, poultry, and legumes.

# Essential Vitamins

Vitamins A and E are two fat-soluble vitamins that contribute to healthy skin and nails. There are two forms of vitamin A. Beta carotene, the best-known form, is found in bright-colored fruits and yellow, orange, and dark green vegetables, including carrots, broccoli, apricots, mangos, cherries, and cantaloupe. The body converts carotene into vitamin A, which helps achieve soft and smooth hands. The second form of vitamin A comes from animal sources such as fish liver oil. Vitamin E is equally important, as it is used to aid in the cleaning and rebuilding of our system to prevent age-spots. Good sources of vitamin E are wheat germ, leafy vegetables, legumes, and vegetable oil.

*Most vegetables and fruit are not only low in calories, but are beneficial for achieving and maintaining healthy hands and nails.*

Biotin, a member of the B-complex family, also helps build healthy, strong nails. Found in cooked egg-yolks, saltwater fish, meat, milk, soybeans, whole grains, and yeast, biotin is known to help strengthen thin and weak nails.

Vitamin C, a well-known antioxidant, may help reduce aging of the skin. Found in citrus fruits, tomatoes, strawberries, potatoes, green peppers, and cabbage, vitamin C also boosts the immune system, making you less susceptible to inflammations and infections. Additionally, connective tissue is fortified by vitamin C, which may also help prevent wrinkling of the skin. Furthermore, vitamin C with bioflavanoids is beneficial for tissue repair.

Calcium and iron are also necessary for nail growth. Calcium is found in food sources such as milk, cheeses, yogurt, and dark green leafy vegetables. Iron deficiencies produce "spoon nails" (bending upward of the nail) and vertical ridges in nails. Iron can be found in eggs, fish, liver, meat, poultry, beans, whole grains, and enriched breads and cereals.

Vitamins and minerals are a fundamental part of healthy living. Hence, it is imperative that you follow the Recommended Daily Allowances (RDA) for vitamins and minerals. It is always best to obtain your vitamin and mineral needs from natural food sources. Always consult with your physician before taking any supplements or herbs.

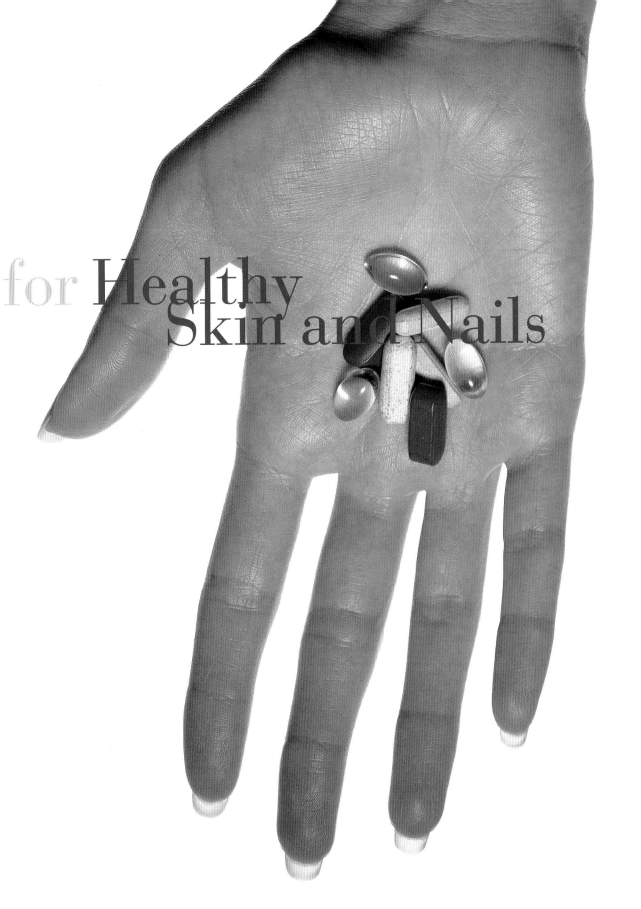

for Healthy
Skin and Nails

# A Perfect Set of Ten

◆ Are your hands a perfect 10?

◆ Are your fingers worth flaunting?

◆ Are your nails long and strong?

◆ Is your skin soft and supple?

Most of us have healthy nails and skin. Keeping them looking good is not a complicated or time-consuming task. For the most part, it simply involves common sense. Maintaining a well-rounded diet, rich in protein, vitamins, and minerals, and protecting nails and skin from the elements are essentials.

*Our polish pick: two coats of classic red creme.*

*Fish is an excellent source of protein.*

*Our polish pick: one coat of pale rose creme and one coat of pale peach pearl.*

# Water, Water, Water

If you begin to notice that your skin is dry and
your nails are brittle, it very well may be the result
of not giving your body enough water. The human
body is composed of 70 percent water. Water is
the primary transporter of nutrients throughout the
body, and is necessary for all the body's functions.
It is essential to drink at least eight glasses of
water daily to properly nourish the skin and nails—
otherwise you run the risk of dehydration.

Healthful eating is key to keeping your skin and nails
in excellent condition. Eat foods from all five food
groups every day in order to meet nutritional require-
ments: milk group for calcium; meat group for protein and iron; vegetable group for vitamin A; fruit
group for vitamin C; and grain group for fiber.

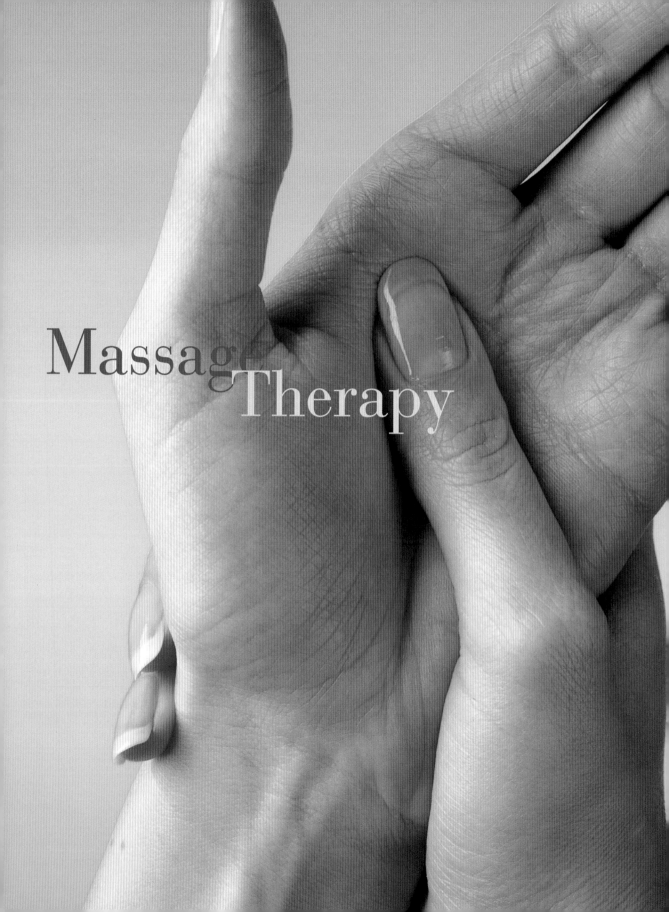

# Massage
# &Therapy

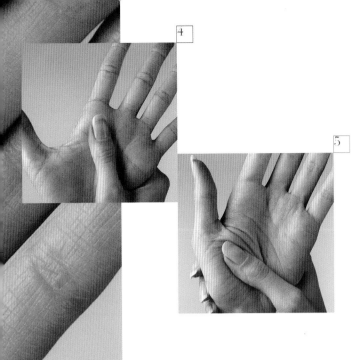

# How to Give Yourself a Million-Dollar Hand Massage

If you suffer from constant cold hands and feet, massage could become your new best friend. If you don't, you can still benefit from massage. Known to stimulate circulation, increase blood flow and metabolism, accelerate toxin removal, decrease blood pressure, and reduce muscle soreness and fatigue, massage is an activity that can make you both mentally and physically feel better.

Step 1 – Start with a massage oil (or lotion) that is mostly paraffin-based and rich in vitamins A, C, and E.

Step 2 – Begin by rubbing the oil (or lotion) on the posterior hand and forearm. Be sure to rub in the direction of the heart to get the circulation moving in the whole arm.

Step 3 – Then knead the hand in a milking fashion. From there, move down to each finger and squeeze, but avoid cracking fingers.

Step 4 – Next, create some deep friction between the metacarpal bones in the hand.

Step 5 – Finish the way you started, by milking the hand and stroking the forearm to help increase the circulation to the whole arm.

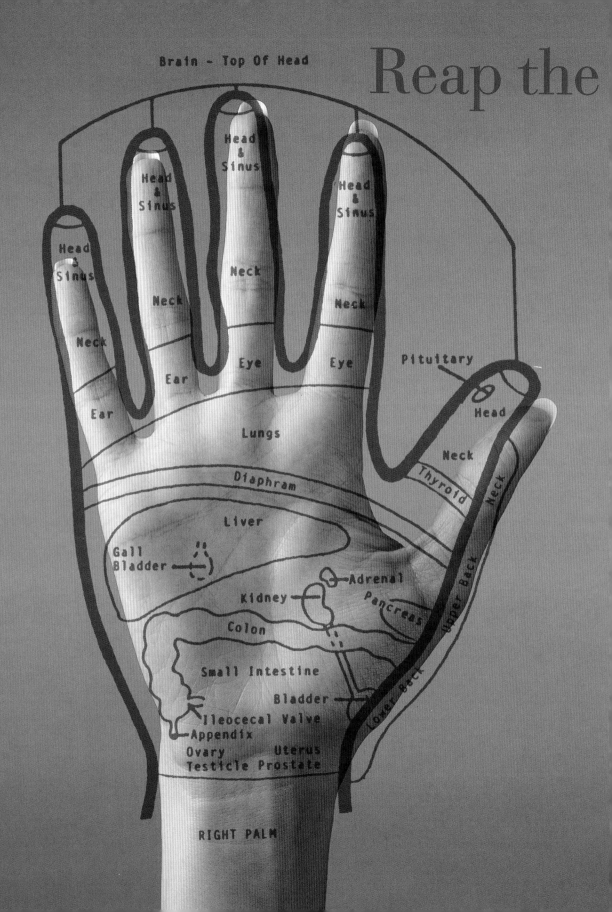

# Rewards
## of Reflexology

## What is Reflexology?

Reflexology is the study of stimulation points, or areas under the skin known as reflexes. Reflexes correspond to specific organs, glands, and structures throughout the body. The motion of properly applying pressure using thumbs and fingers to the points is known as reflexing. It is not, however, intended to be used as a substitute for medical treatment.

Reflexing can relieve energy blockages in the hands. Deeply relaxing, reflexing helps reduce the effects of stress on the body and emotions. It is a way of providing caring, pampering, attention, compassion, understanding, and acceptance, as well as direct and indirect benefits to the body itself. Reflexing can also be used to encourage nail growth and strengthening.

## Benefits of Reflexology

**To strengthen nails, try this easy exercise:**

Step 1 – Rub the fingernails from one hand directly across the other hand, with a quick rapid motion as if you were buffing them.

Step 2 – Do this simple exercise for five minutes or more, three times a day. This technique will enhance nail growth.

◆ Improves circulation – in the hands as well as the rest of the body.

◆ Reduces aches and pains.

◆ Normalizes body functions – slows down an overactive organ, gland, or structure of the body, or brings up to normal an underactive one.

◆ Detoxes – releases toxins from the hand as well as the whole body.

◆ Profoundly relaxes.

◆ Reduces effects of stress.

Reflexology involves a safe, non-intrusive form of touch, and it is a natural and drugless therapy. An estimated 90 percent of all imbalances are stress-related. We can minimize the unhealthy stress in our life with reflexology.

# RX:
## Remedies for Hand and Nail Problems

### The Most Common Hand and Nail Problems

### Hangnails and Infected Cuticles

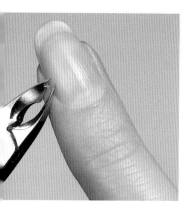

Hangnails involve a small tear or split in the skin around the nail edges and can be quite painful. Very dry skin, an injury on or around the nails, nail biting, and excessive picking are all common causes of hangnails. If not cared for properly, they can become infected. The nail should be kept clean and covered with a Band-Aid. Once grown out sufficiently, it should be carefully clipped.

Infected cuticles are often a result of aggressive manicures, nervous picking, or a direct consequence of an injury to the nail area. The skin around the nail often becomes tender, red, swollen, and, in cases of severe infection, large accumulations of puss can develop in the skin. Prevention is the key approach: cuticles should never be cut or pushed aggressively with a sharp instrument. At the earliest sign of infection—redness, tenderness, or swelling—the finger should be soaked for approximately ten minutes in an antimicrobial solution such as Burows Solution or 5 percent acetic acid, and topical antibiotic ointment applied after allowing the skin to air-dry.

If symptoms do not subside (i.e., swelling, redness, and/or pain persists), consult a physician. Systemic antibiotics may be necessary.

### Mold and Fungus

Mold and fungus usually appear one of two ways: as thickened, discolored nails with much debris under the free edge of the nail, or separation of the nail plate from the nail bed, which usually results in a white discoloration.

*Olive oil is especially soothing for dry, cracked cuticles. (See page 38 for using oil in parrafin treatment.)*

Early recognition and prompt treatment are crucial. Nails should be kept short and clean. Since moisture is a fertile ground for Candida (yeast) to grow, hands should be dried thoroughly with special attention to fingernails. There are a wide variety of topical "antifungals" available to control fungus and yeast infections. Often these products possess antibacterial properties as well. If there is no response, or if the fungus infection progresses, topical or systemic medication may be required. A dermatologist can examine and culture the affected nail and determine the best treatment.

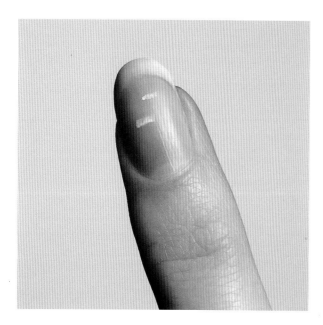

## Trauma Spots and Horizontal Ridges

Trauma spots are a result of repeated trauma to the fingernail and can be manifested in a variety of ways:

◆ When the nail or nail bed is physically injured, the resulting nail can show the evidence of this trauma.

◆ Nervous picking or pushing at the base of the cuticle will result in a nail plate that has a series of central horizontal grooves and depressions running down the nail.

◆ Shortly after trauma in a particular area (known as subungual hematomas), blood can accumulate underneath the fingernail. As the nail grows out, the pocket of blood will resolve.

"Beau's Lines" refer to the horizontal ridges or lines seen on fingernails and toenails. They are historical indicators of "events" that took place at the time the nail was forming. These "events" can include illnesses with high fevers, zinc deficiency, and trauma resulting from aggressive cuticle-pushing during manicuring.

## Dermatitis

Inflammation of the skin is known as dermatitis. When applied to hands, it refers to redness, itching, flaking, and/or dryness, and can be caused from the following:

◆ Contact eczema is the result of an allergy to a topical agent to which the hands may have been exposed. These can include creams, chemicals, soaps, nail polishes, or hair-care products.

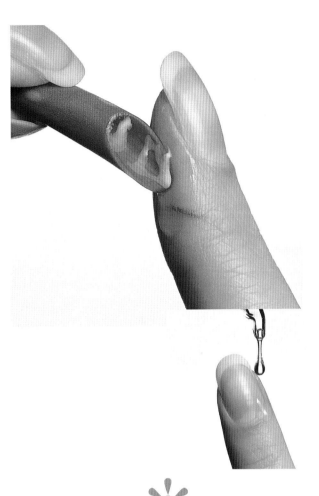

◆ Hand eczema is a chronic condition that causes recurring eruptions of redness, itching, thickened skin, flaking, and sometimes blisters. Avoidance of extended exposure to water, chemicals, and irritants, as well as frequent moisturizing, helps keep eczema under control. Topical cortisones that can be prescribed by a dermatologist may be necessary in certain instances.

## Dry Nails and Splitting

Dry nails and splitting can be caused by outside factors like having hands in water too often or certain nail glues. This condition can also result from certain diseases or drug therapy. Some easy treatments are a warm olive oil soak, topical alpha hydroxy acid (AHA) application, nail conditioners, and wearing gloves when hands are exposed to water for an extended period of time.

## Age-Spots

Age-spots can be treated conservatively with topical bleaching or lightening creams. These contain hydroquinone, a safe lightening agent. When used in combination with a topical over-the-counter AHA, the treatment time can be significantly reduced. For age-spots that have been present for many years and seem resistant to over-the-counter products, a consultation with a dermatologist may be beneficial. Age-spots and freckles can be treated by a number of modalities including lasers, freezing, or chemical peeling.

### Trick of our trade

For painful paper cuts, try blow-drying the cut. After, add aloe or vitamin E for their healing benefits.

# NAILS 101

More and more women are choosing to perform beauty treatments, such as facials, waxing, tweezing, and manicures, in the privacy–and comfort–of their own homes. Whether it's steaming, removing, or polishing, each of these tasks can be done easily at your leisure. In fact, giving yourself a manicure is often the most relaxing and self-indulgent way to spend an hour. If you know how, it's simple. If you don't, we're here to explore and explain the fundamentals. From A to Z, here is your complete guide on how to give yourself a manicure at home–and enjoy doing it.

*Our polish pick: two coats of hot pink creme.*

The Perfect Manicure

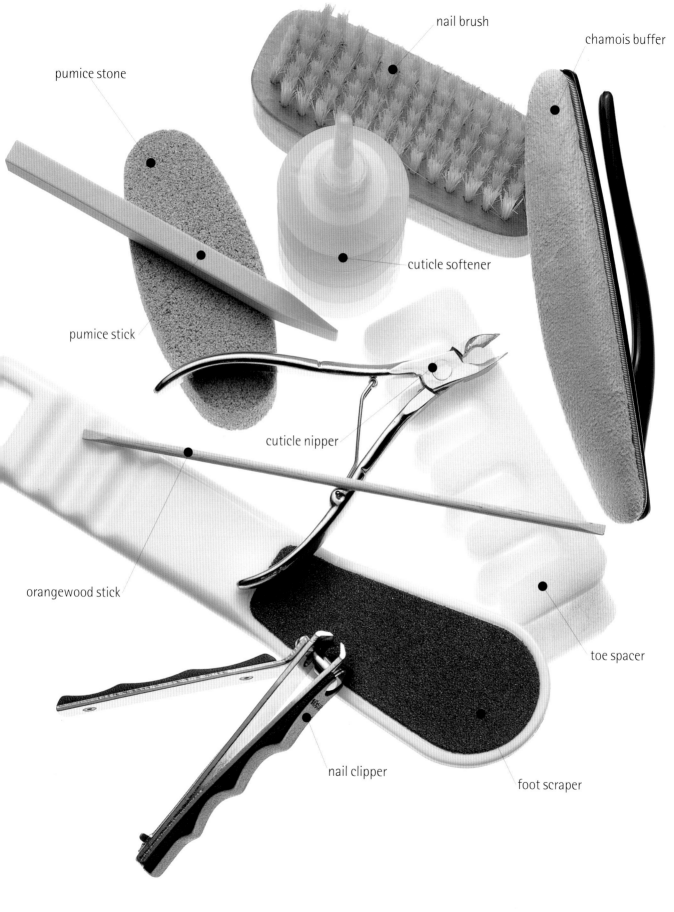

nail brush

chamois buffer

pumice stone

cuticle softener

pumice stick

cuticle nipper

orangewood stick

toe spacer

nail clipper

foot scraper

# Supplies for Success

## Nailing down the basics and getting into the mood

Your basic manicure really is quite simple, provided you follow these easy instructions. First and foremost, reserve approximately one hour. Create a peaceful environment. Take your phone off the hook and put on your favorite music. If you really want to indulge, try lighting a scented candle. Now take a deep breath and relax.

## Comfort is everything

Whether it's blue jeans and a T-shirt, flannel pajamas and fuzzy slippers, or a silky negligee, get comfortable. Once your body is unrestricted, find an equally comfortable space to work. Make sure it's well-lit and clean with a spacious, hard surface. While polishing your nails, be very careful not to sit under direct light, such as a lamp. The close light will cause the polish to bubble. Also, avoid direct drafts, fans, air conditioners, and heaters, as these will also cause polish bubbling.

**Trick of our trade**

Do not store polish in a warm place or in direct sunlight – the polish will change consistency. Always keep polish in a cool, dark place such as the refrigerator or a dark cabinet.

# Supply List for the Perfect Manicure

**base coat polish and top coat polish**

If nails are weak, use a ridge filler as the base coat for priming and a nail hardening top coat to secure longevity of the polish and give it a shiny finish.

**buffing disc**

A very fine-grade sandpaper on a round disc with a thin cushion in the center. Used to smooth off rough nail edges or to buff the surface of the nail.

**cotton balls**

Only 100 percent cotton will do.

**cuticle nipper**

To be used for trimming hangnails only.

**cuticle softener**

Softens cuticles, making them easy to push back.

**emery board**

Has two sides. Use the fine side for smoothing edges, and the rough for shortening nail extensions. Never use a metal one!

**hand cream**

This is one area that you should not skimp on. The more you use, the softer your hands will be.

**nail brush**

Preferably extra soft. An old toothbrush also works well for removing difficult dirt, especially under nail tips.

**nail polish**

This is where your individual taste and lifestyle come into play. Nail color can be a decorative enhancement when you wear a natural, sheer color or a classic red. On the contrary, if you choose dark eggplant, metallic brown, or bright purple, you're sure to make a personal statement. Whichever shade you choose, nail color is all about self-expression. Decide what suits you and go with it.

**nail polish remover**

Your best bet is a remover with a conditioner, such as vitamin E, lanolin, or aloe, which are all less drying to the nail. If your skin is classified as extremely sensitive, use a non-acetone remover.

**orangewood stick**

For gently pushing back cuticles and cleaning around the nail. Never use a metal pusher—it is too harsh.

**soft towel**

Great for leaning on and drying hands.

**warm soapy water**

To loosen dirt from under nails and soften cuticles, making them much easier to push back.

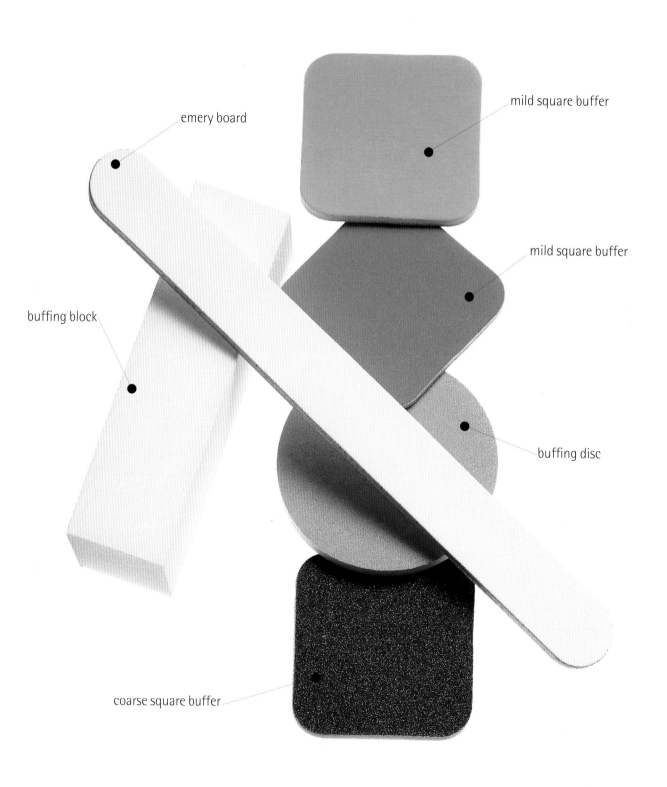

emery board

mild square buffer

mild square buffer

buffing block

buffing disc

coarse square buffer

# A Step-by-Step Guide to the Perfect Manicure

**Step 1—cleaning:** Once you have assembled all of your tools and you're relaxed. it's time to begin. First things first – start with a thorough hand wash. Be sure to dry hands completely.

**Step 2—filing:** File nails. Avoid filing deep in the corners and always use a gentle stroke. Double-sided emery boards are the best choice: one side is smooth; the other, a bit coarser. If your nails are just beginning to grow, do not attempt to shape them. Just simply buff off rough edges with a mild buffing disc.

**Step 3—shaping:** Use the shape of your nail base as a guide—most are oval. If you prefer a more square shape. rounding out nail edges will achieve this dramatic shape.

2

*Nail shapes (from left to right): rounded-square, oval, and square. Our polish pick: two coats of classic red.*

3

**Step 4—hosiery test:** When you are through filing and shaping, take the hosiery test! Run your nails over an old pair of hosiery to check for any rough edges. It's a surefire way to hone in on hard-to-see rough spots.

**Step 5—cuticles:** Apply cuticle softener around cuticles. Then place hands in warm soapy water. Depending on the condition of your cuticles, let hands soak for three to five minutes—the thicker your cuticles are, the longer you will need to soak them. Use a nail brush to remove dirt around and under nails.

**For dry cuticles only:** If your cuticles are severely dry and cracked (most tend to be during the cold, harsh winter), you may want to try a lactol (creamy lotion) manicure, olive oil, or cuticle oil warmed in a special heater. (A heater can be purchased in any beauty supply store, or you can use a microwave.) After just a few treatments, you will definitely see an improvement in overall skin dryness. If you do opt for the lactol manicure, simply use it instead of soaking hands in warm soapy water.

Remove hands from warm soapy water or from the cream in the lactol manicure. Then gently push back cuticles. If you have any hangnails, use your cuticle nipper to remove them. When you use the nipper, direct it towards yourself and gently nip. Use an orangewood stick to remove any dirt under the nails. Again, be very gentle.

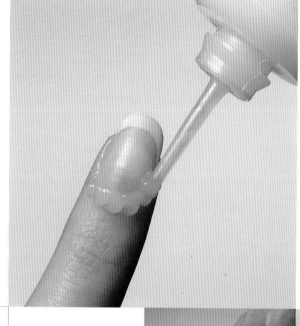

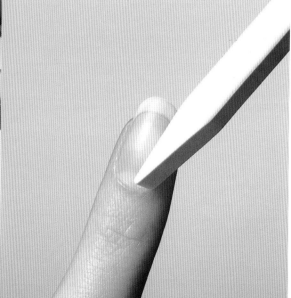

Step 6—massage: Most say that this is truly the best part! Lube up with hand lotion and rotate with your thumb on the inside of you hand to circulate the blood flow. Massage both your hands and arms. This is the time to really pamper yourself, so use as much lotion as you want and massage for as long as you like.

If you have severely dry skin, a paraffin hand treatment is a good idea. Paraffin is a moisturizing wax that can be melted in its own special heater. Dip both hands in, then take them out and let the paraffin dry and harden. Once it hardens, remove the wax by peeling it off. This wonderful treatment is sure to make your hands moist and supple. You can purchase paraffin heaters at most beauty supply stores. A heater is a bit costly, but well worth the investment. Or you can heat paraffin in a double boiler. Be sure to test a small area of skin to make sure it's not too hot before applying it to the entire hand.

6

7

8

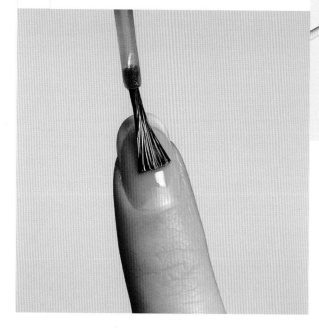

Step 7—final cleaning: Clean the surface and the back of the nail with your cotton-wrapped orangewood stick dipped in nail polish remover. Rub over the entire nail surface making sure that there is no remaining creamy residue—otherwise nail polish will not adhere to the surface. Now you're ready for the base coat or if needed, ridge filler. After applying, wait one minute before moving on to color.

Step 8—color application: Make sure there is not a lot of polish on the brush. Apply color with a light stroke. Begin in the center of the nail at the base and brush quickly. Then stroke down each side. Unless you're using a "one-coat" polish, wait one minute before applying the second coat. To clean up any polish residue, use the orangewood stick dipped in remover to wipe away excess. When polish is dry to touch (usually ten to fifteen minutes), apply a top coat. The top coat is very important—so don't skip it! In addition to lengthening the life of a manicure, the top coat gives nails a beautiful shine. There are many varieties to choose from—fast-drying, strengthening, and extra shine, among others.

**Trick of our trade**

If this is your first time, or you're in a big hurry, it is best to use a light-color polish. No major goof-ups will show with a light color!

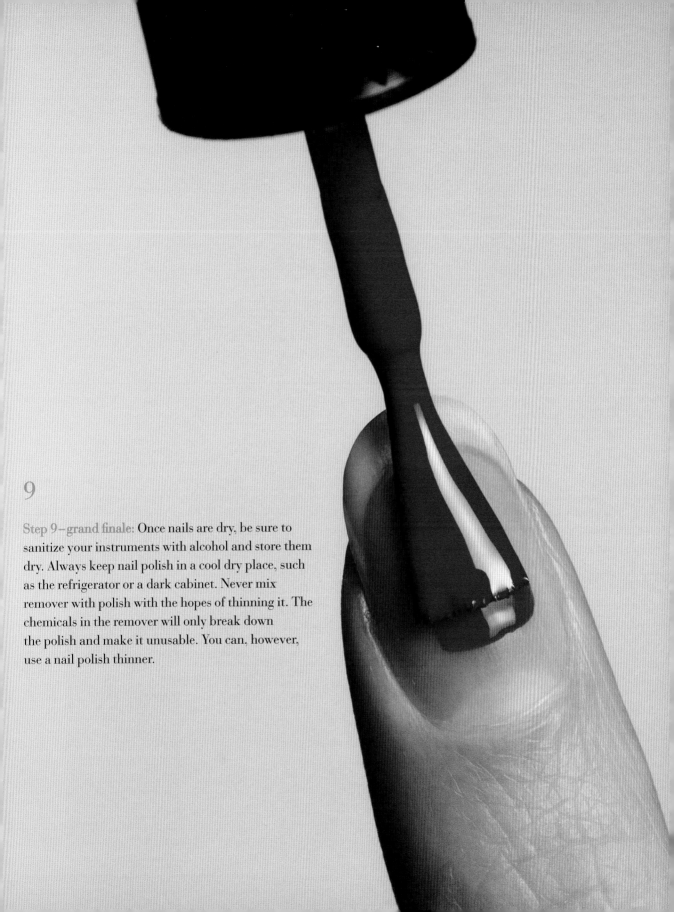

9

Step 9–grand finale: Once nails are dry, be sure to
sanitize your instruments with alcohol and store them
dry. Always keep nail polish in a cool dry place, such
as the refrigerator or a dark cabinet. Never mix
remover with polish with the hopes of thinning it. The
chemicals in the remover will only break down
the polish and make it unusable. You can, however,
use a nail polish thinner.

# The Grand Finale

*Our polish pick: two coats
of violet stain.*

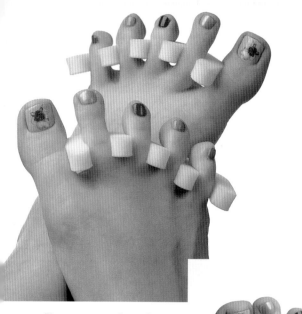

# The Perfect Pedicure

*Toe spacers make pedicures a breeze.*

*Our polish pick (from left to right): two coats of lime green creme with rose decal, two coats of orange creme, two coats of red creme, two coats of turquoise creme, and two coats of true pink creme.*

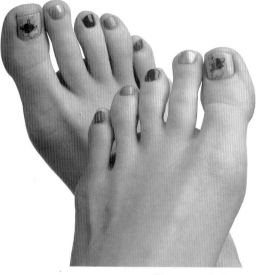

Beautiful, well-groomed feet are just as important as beautiful hands—especially in the warmer weather, when feet tend to be exposed more. To give yourself the perfect pedicure, follow the same simple steps for a manicure with a few exceptions.

♦ Use toenail clippers to cut toenails straight across.

♦ Then use an emery board to smooth off rough edges.

♦ When applying polish, always use toe separators to keep toes apart.

♦ And remember, if you always played it safe with sheer, pale polish on your fingernails, your feet are the perfect place to experiment with brighter, darker polish. Have fun with colors, decals, and even a toe ring. No one else has to know what's hiding under your conservative business shoes!

**Trick of our trade**

Feet and legs have little or no oil glands and need to be moisturized twice as often. The best time to apply moisturizer is after bathing for faster absorption.

# The Manly Manicure

Men can sometimes be a bit squeamish when it comes to a manicure. They don't always realize they need a manicure until they're told and then are usually reluctant to get one. Instead of presenting it as a "chore" or a "duty," try explaining it as a pampering luxury. Once they have their first, they're guaranteed to love it and are sure to come back for more.

A basic man's manicure is very similar to a woman's manicure with three exceptions:

◆ Nail length should be short with a tiny amount of white "free edge" showing. Nothing is more unattractive than a man with long nails.

◆ Shaping must always follow the same shape of the nail base. Very few men request a different shape.

◆ A buffed look, as opposed to clear polish, is much more sophisticated. However, if a man is experimental, he can certainly wear dark polish. In fact, there is a whole line of nail polish made specifically for men with dark colors that resemble car paint. If this concept is unappealing, buff nails with a chamois buffer and buffing cream that contains a gentle abrasive. After applying the cream, stroke twenty times per nail. Finish with a relaxing and pampering hand massage.

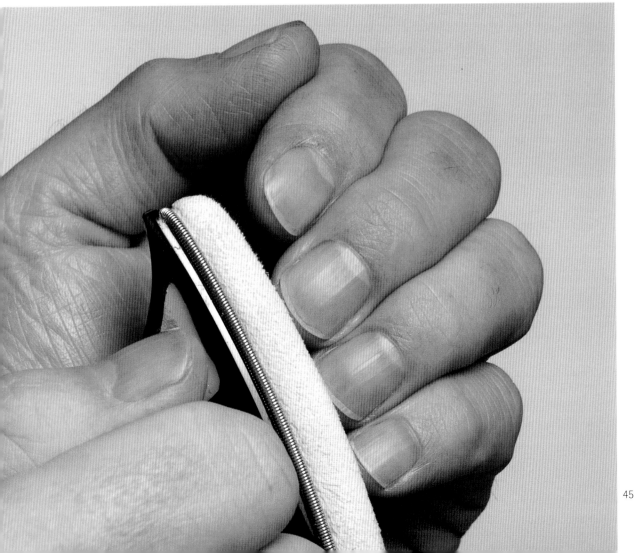

# Manicures for the Under-Twelve Set

If you're able to get a child to sit still, you've accomplished half the job. A child's manicure is very similar to a woman's manicure without the cuticle nipper and rough emery board. Instead, use only children's scissors and an extra soft emery board. It's important to remember to *never* cut their little cuticles. Use a non-acetone remover for its gentleness. If possible, avoid colors with glitter because they're next to impossible to remove. Lastly, always be very careful and patient when working with children's hands.

# Breaking the Nail Biting Habit

Granted, it's one of the hardest habits to break, but once you do, you'll reap the benefits with beautiful hands and nails. First, it's imperative to make the mental commitment to stop biting. Once you've done that, give yourself a manicure every four days. Pay special attention to cuticles. This is the one and only time that it's okay to cut cuticles. The reason? It leaves you with nothing left to bite! Buff out the rough edges and apply one coat of clear polish every day. Wait four days, remove, and start over. Repeat this for two months.

**How will you stop biting?**
Pick one finger (preferably the pinky) and don't bite that nail for one month. Feel free to bite the other nine nails morning, noon, and night. During the second month, don't bite the pinky and the ring finger. Remember, it's still okay to bite the other eight nails. Each month, add another nail. Sometime in the next ten months you should be a recovered nail biter forever.

# Beauty Masks for Hands and Feet

Most of us perform masks on our faces monthly, or even weekly. The skin on our hands and feet can certainly benefit from similar treatment. The following masks are simple and can be done at home:

**Hand Helpers**

◆ Smooth four teaspoons of honey on your hands and let dry for fifteen minutes. This will soften and moisturize skin. Wash thoroughly with very warm water, dry, and put on your favorite hand cream.

◆ Mix six teaspoons of oatmeal, six teaspoons of plain yogurt, one tablespoon of olive oil, and two tablespoons of lemon juice in a bowl. Smooth on hands for ten minutes and then rinse off. If used repeatedly, it will even out a fading tan with its mild bleaching effect as it sloughs off dry skin.

◆ In a large bowl, add one-half cup of powdered whole milk, one tablespoon of castor oil, five drops of lavender, and five drops of chamomile. Run very warm water into the bowl. Swish around with your hands, then soak until the water cools.

# Extra Treats for the Feet

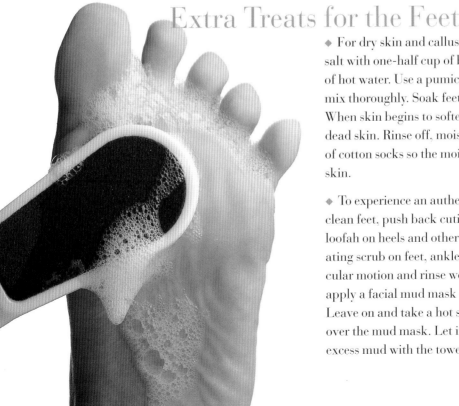

◆ For dry skin and calluses add one-half cup of coarse salt with one-half cup of baking soda in a shallow tub of hot water. Use a pumice stone or a callus scraper to mix thoroughly. Soak feet for ten to fifteen minutes. When skin begins to soften, use a scrubber to remove dead skin. Rinse off, moisturize, and put on a pair of cotton socks so the moisturizer will absorb into the skin.

◆ To experience an authentic Hawaiian pedicure, clean feet, push back cuticles, buff toenails, and use a loofah on heels and other dry skin areas. Use an exfoliating scrub on feet, ankles, and legs. Massage in a circular motion and rinse well in warm water. Then apply a facial mud mask onto legs, ankles, and feet. Leave on and take a hot steamed towel and place it over the mud mask. Let it set for ten minutes. Wipe off excess mud with the towel and rinse well.

**Trick of our trade**

At bedtime, wash hands thoroughly and towel-dry, leaving skin slightly damp. Slather on a rich, moisturizing cream. Put on cotton gloves and go to sleep. This overnight treatment is the quickest way to relieve dry, chapped hands. For significant improvement, try this for a few consecutive nights.

## Color Explosion

For as long as we can remember, nail polish was quite simple. Women had a few choices: basic sheer, classic red, and a handful of pinks. But that has all changed – and changed dramatically. After years of floundering in a sea of peaches and cream, it was only a matter of time before nail polish shifted in an entirely new direction. Today, women are not only waking up to endless shade possibilities—they're demanding them. From white to black to everything in between, nail color has become a creative form of individuality and self-expression.

Just like a classic handbag, a good shoe, or a fine piece of jewelry, nail polish is an essential accessory, as well as a surefire way to make a statement. In this chapter, we will help you make the right statement by identifying the best shades for you along with expert tips for application, layering, and removal. From shimmer to metallic to glitter, a woman with beautifully polished nails is the epitome of style.

M

Our polish pick: two coats of
bright yellow pearl with red
angled stripe.

Just like the clothes you wear, the nail polish shades you select reflect your individual style. Trends change. If you were around during the fifties, you may remember that it was cool to wear red polish. In the sixties you were considered a groovy gal if you wore white pearl polish. The seventies were the decade of psychedelic brights. In the eighties it was chic to sport no-nonsense, sheer polish. The nineties have brought a myriad of extremes and a fabulous explosion of color.

## A Sign of the Times

With regard to physical appearance, it is easy to get stuck in a rut. If you're wearing your hair and make-up the same as you did in high school, it's time to make some style adjustments. The perfect place to begin is with your nails. As we prepare to enter the new millennium, there have never been so many options. Shade possibilities are endless.

When women began to enter the workforce some forty years ago, they were expected to blend in a male-dominated population. Somber suits, tailored blouses, understated hair, make-up, and nails were the norm. Fortunately, times have changed. The glass ceiling is lifting as women everywhere demonstrate their own individual style. In fact, men are taking note of our good grooming habits. From bronzers to plastic surgery to nail polish, men have never paid more attention to their own physical appearance.

## The Changing

teal pearl

deep purple confetti

purple pearl

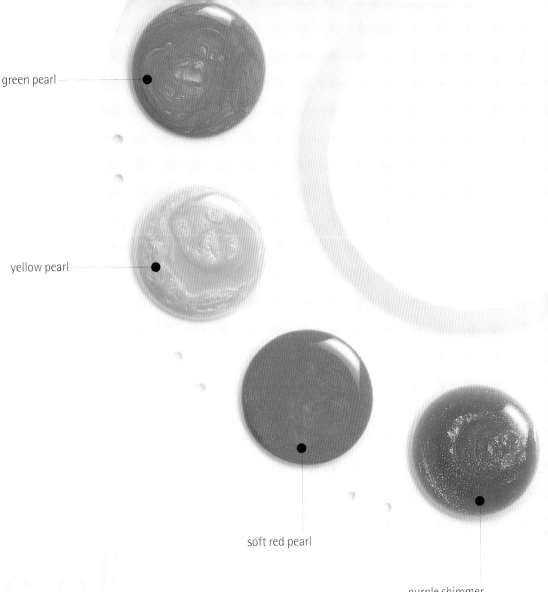

green pearl

yellow pearl

soft red pearl

purple shimmer

It started in 1995 when a famous cosmetic company introduced a very dark berry nail polish that quickly became the rage from coast to coast. From teenagers to grandmothers—it was an influential crowd-pleaser. It was chic, it was "French," it was oh, so fabulous. Every nail polish company copied it, causing a phenomenal domino effect. Each company created more extraordinary colors than the next. Nails began to look like an artist's palette: yellow, red, blue, green, purple, orange, black, white, gray – some pearlized, others glittery. From the banker on Wall Street to the supermarket checkout girl, creative expression with nail polish reached staggering proportions.

# Polish Up Your Act

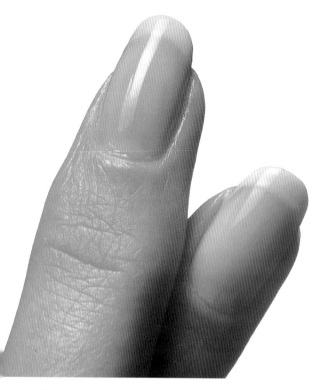

Whether you're at home or work, manicured nails look and feel good. Unlike a chic new haircut or a great new lip liner, perfectly groomed hands and nails give you a constant lift because they are often within your own eyesight. Seeing a flash of color wave before your eyes has an instant uplifting effect. Brightly colored nails can make you giddy, and decals on your toes can make you silly. Whatever look you are trying to achieve, we can help you get there.

First and foremost, always use a base coat. It provides a smooth surface for polish.

If your look is subtle, wear a sheer color. Sheers are translucent and range in colors, including white, cream, pink, beige, coral, lavender, and peach. Easy to apply and simple to clean up, sheer polish is classic. Layering sheer colors will give you a more opaque finish. Experiment with one, two, or three coats, depending on the desired texture.

**Trick of our trade**

The darker and brighter the color, the more maintenance required. Never wear chipped polish – it sends the wrong message. Keep polish handy for repairs. Smooth the chip with a buffing disc; fill in with color; then apply a top coat to extend the length of your manicure.

*Our polish pick: two coats of sheer pink with a pale white tip.*

# Sheers

*Our polish pick: two coats of
pale pink creme.*

# Nail Stains

Nail stains are to the nails what lip gloss is to the lips. Giving off a hint of glossy color, nail stains look undeniably modern. Just like a deep, dark lipstick is hard to maintain, so is a deep, dark nail polish. That's why nail stains are the perfect answer – intense color without the heavy pigment. They're clear and glossy with a touch of color, including red, dark berry, violet, orange, or pink. You can make your own by adding a few drops of a richly pigmented basic creme polish into a bottle of clear polish. Then shake well for your very own nail stain! Experiment with one to three coats of nail stain, depending on your personal preference.

# Shimmers

Shimmer polish is a sheer polish containing pearl or opalescent flecks. It can be worn with one or two coats. Or for a slight variation, layer one coat of sheer polish with one coat of coordinating shimmer polish (i.e., sheer beige with gold shimmer, sheer lavender with opal shimmer) for a smashing look.

Metallic shades are blends of creme formulations with a bronze, gold, silver, or copper effect. Frost shades are blends of basic creme formulations with pearl polish. Stylish jewel-tone reds (bright or deep), rich pinks, corals, bold oranges, and fuchsias look beautiful on anyone, at any age, at any time. They are available in basic creme, metallic, and frost formulations. When applying jewel-toned colors, be extra careful that there is not too much polish on the brush or it will spill onto the cuticles during application. Because these colors are extremely rich in pigment, always use a ridge-filling base coat to prevent staining on the nails.

# Metallics Frosts

*Our polish pick: two coats of white frost.*

Our polish pick: two coats of rust pearl and two coats of rust glitter.

Jewel-Tones

# Freedom of Expression

Just like clothing and make-up, nail polish can be worn alone or in layers. Here are a few ideas for layering:

◆ Start off with a creme formula in red and add a multicolored glitter.

◆ Start off with a creme formula in black and add a gold glitter.

◆ Start off with a creme formula in blue and add a purple glitter.

◆ Start off with a creme formula in gray and add a burgundy glitter.

◆ Start off with a creme formula in yellow and add an orange glitter.

*Our polish pick: two coats of red creme and one coat of red and gold glitter.*

◆ Try two different colors on each nail. Put on two coats of a bright red polish and let dry for ten to fifteen minutes. Then, using an eyeliner brush for easy application, paint the tip yellow. Try black and gray – darker on the bottom; lighter on the top.

*Our polish pick: one coat of teal creme on tips with two coats of opal sky blue creme over the entire nail.*

◆ Paint each nail a different color in the same family (i.e., all primary colors: blue, yellow, green, orange, purple), and your hands will look like crayons. Or try deep metallics (i.e., burgundy, dark violet, black, navy blue, forest green) for a mysterious, opulent look.

*Our polish pick: two coats of each: teal, green, purple, burnt umber, purple, yellow/green copper, deep burgundy, soft gold/green and brown.*

Another hot trend-of-the-moment is confetti polish. It's like glitter polish but the flecks are much larger and therefore, more dramatic. For pure drama, try the following:

◆ Use two coats of a jewel-toned creme formula under two coats of confetti polish in a contrasting color.

◆ For a 3-D look: use one coat of sheer (i.e., pale pink), then one coat of glimmer in opal, and finish off with one coat of pink glitter. Make sure each coat is dry to the touch before applying the next coat.

*Our polish pick: two coats each of pink fuchsia creme, white opal, red creme, blue opal, lavender opal, and two coats of corresponding confetti polish on each nail.*

**Trick of our trade**

If you want to darken a polish, add a few drops of black polish. If you want to lighten a polish, add a few drops of white polish, and shake thoroughly.

| Hot Tip | You may want to experiment with some of these color statements on your toes to see if you like them before polishing your nails.

Icy Blue Polish Sets Off A Hand Embellished With Diamonds.

*Our polish pick: two coats of royal blue pearl.*

# Long-Lasting Manicure and Pedicure

A manicure will last approximately four to seven days. A pedicure will last approximately ten to fifteen days. Nails are like sponges. They expand when wet and contract when dry. Therefore, when your hands are in and out of water (i.e., washing, bathing, cleaning), they are constantly expanding and contracting, making it very difficult for nail polish to stay on. That's why a pedicure will last longer than a manicure, and polish on artificial nails rarely chips.

*Our polish pick: two coats of blood red creme.*

### Trick of our trade

When removing a dark-color nail polish, let the cotton ball sit on the nail for a few seconds to loosen the polish.

# Color Coordinated

Be careful to coordinate nail polish and lipstick. They certainly don't have to match exactly. However, they should blend rather than clash. For example, avoid orange metallic nails with fuchsia creme lips.

## The Nineties Version of a Masculine Manicure

*Our polish pick: two coats of indigo blue.*

The dark metallics and deep primary colors have recently developed a prominent following among men from Gen-Xers to rockers to any guy who simply wants to have some fun. Most colors resemble car paint or those used to decorate model airplanes. In fact, there are even a few lines of nail polish made exclusively for men that are selling quite well. Men should follow the same guidelines as women:

◆ Nail polish can look great, until it chips. It needs to be maintained (see page 54).

◆ Men, like women, should always use a base coat and a top coat to extend the life of the manicure and pedicure.

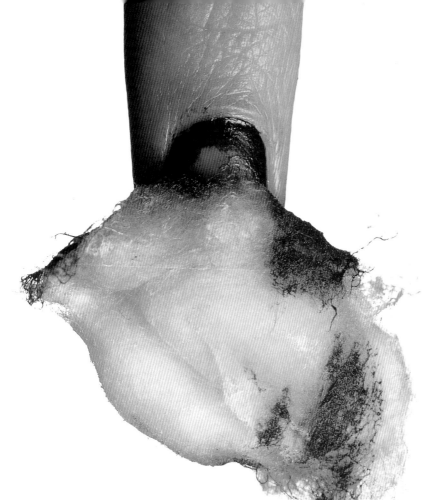

# Take it All Off

◆ Use only 100 percent cotton balls for removing polish. Smaller size cotton balls are recommended. If you use synthetic cotton with remover, the fibers will break down and residue will be left on the nail beds. This will ultimately lead to tiny particles in the polish. We suggest one cotton ball per nail. If you're removing light or sheer nail color, non-acetone remover is great. But if you're wearing a dark, rich color, get serious and use a remover with acetone.

Step 1– Wet the cotton ball with remover but don't saturate.

**Trick of our trade**

Don't buy nail polish because of price or packaging. Choose polish for color and quality.

Step 2 – Place cotton ball on the fingernail, then wipe away from the nail. Do not go back and forth, or you will get polish in the cuticles.

◆ Confetti and other glitter polishes are very difficult to remove. Pour remover into its cap and soak each nail individually until the polish softens. Then wet a cotton ball and remove.

Step 3– After you're done, always rinse nails in warm water to wash off any nail polish remover residue. Then moisturize.

# Nailing Down the Facts on Longevity, Storage, Prices

◆ Nail polish has a shelf life of approximately one to two years, especially if it is kept in a cool, dark place and the lids are closed tightly. Store in the refrigerator or on a closet floor. If your polish thickens, try a few drops of nail polish thinner (not remover) to extend the life of your favorite polish. If it separates or becomes too thick, throw it out.

◆ The price of a bottle of nail polish ranges from two dollars to fifteen dollars. Most formulations are identical and are made by the same chemists with a few exceptions. Some polishes contain more pigment, making them richer in intensity. Be careful of an extremely thick polish, as it will streak easily. It's a good idea to test the polish on your nails before purchasing. If it's a creme formulation, it should give you 50 to 75 percent coverage with the first coat. If it's a sheer polish, check for streaking.

**Hot Tip**

When you're in a hurry (i.e., a last-minute date or unexpected warm weather, and your toes have been hiding in winter boots) the new fast-drying polishes are a great option. They contain ingredients that help them dry quickly, but they don't usually last as long as other formulations. Therefore, use two coats of top coat to extend the life of your manicure.

# Make-believe

Whether children play doctor, school, or dress-up, most enjoy an innocent game of "make-believe." If we stop to think about it, adults too, often play make-believe. Every time we attach false eyelashes, wear a padded bra, or color our brown hair blonde, we are essentially "making-believe." And why not? These minor transformations have the ability to make us feel confident, relaxed, and pretty.

If the very idea of a permanent change makes you uncomfortable, why not try something fun that requires minimal commitment? Dressing up hands and nails can be the easiest way to lift your spirits and feel good about yourself. From nail extensions to beautiful decals to Mehndi (the ancient Middle Eastern art), we will help you make sense of the options, teach you how to create special effects – and have fun experimenting!

*Our polish pick: two coats of light purple opal with a hologram decal on top.*

With today's advanced technology, everyone can have the perfect ten. Because there are so many cosmetic companies manufacturing nail extension kits, choosing the best product and process for your individual needs can be rather confusing. Whether it's building a full set of nails, adding a protective coat to your own nails, or repairing a broken nail, we will lead the way through with a step-by-step guide.

# Repairs

One way to mend a broken nail is with a basic nail wrap. You can either buy a nail repair kit or make do with what you have at home. Take either a piece of white silk, linen, a coffee filter, or a tea bag and cut into a small square. Make sure it is big enough to fit over the break in your nail. Always begin with the pinky when doing all ten fingers. This type of wrap should last approximately four weeks. If it starts to lift off sooner, add a few drops of glue on the lifted area and let dry and buff.

## How To: Basic Nail Wrap

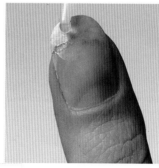

1
If you have a crack in the nail, glue the nail crack together.

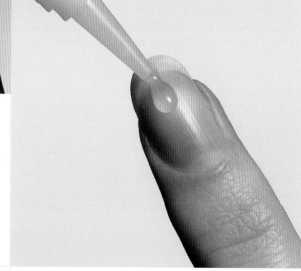

**Trick of our trade**

Always carry a tea bag, nipper, and glue in your purse for emergency repairs! This tip especially comes in handy at the airport after carrying heavy luggage!

2
Apply glue on one-third of the nail tip. Be very careful not to put on too much glue, as you don't want it to seep into cuticles.

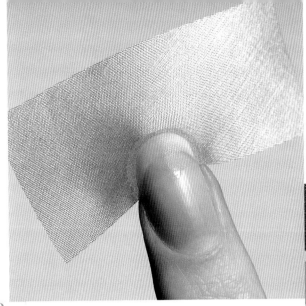

**3**

Place white silk, linen, a coffee filter, or tea bag over one-third of the glue-covered nail and hold the material down for a few seconds on top of the glue and let dry. Do not wrap extra fabric around and under the nail.

**4**

Apply glue on top of the entire nail. When material hardens, the glue is dry. File excess material off the edges of the nail.

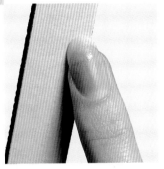

**5**

Use a buffing disc or file to buff the glue on the surface until it is smooth.

**6**

Add a drop or two of glue to the surface and let dry. Buff again until perfectly smooth so that you can't tell where the nail wrap ends and the uncovered nail begins.

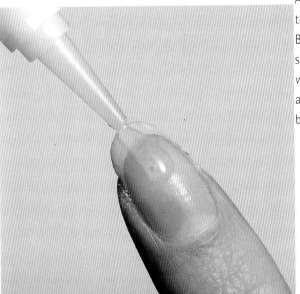

# Nail Extensions

Applying acetate tips over your nails is one way to lengthen them. The tips come in all shapes, sizes, and lengths. Your best option is the "active length" which is average to normal. Acetate tips certainly look good, but unfortunately are not very strong. Therefore, they don't tend to last too long. However, the shorter they are, the longer they'll last.

One way to extend the life of acetate tips is to add a wrap to each nail. Follow the directions for a basic nail wrap, only cut the material bigger so that it fits over the top half of each nail. You can also preserve the manicure by applying a layer of sculptured acrylic nails over the tips. This not only makes nails strong, it will prevent nail polish from chipping. (See next section for how to create sculptured acrylic nails.)

## How To: Acetate Tips

1 Choose a nail tip that fits the width of your nail.

2 If you can't find a tip that fits exactly, take one that is slightly wider and file down the sides so it fits perfectly.

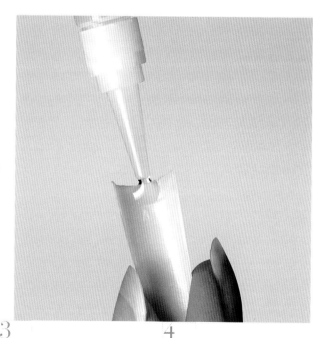

**Trick of our trade**

Use a ridge-filling base coat when nails are tipped or wrapped for a smooth nail base to apply nail color on.

3 Apply one drop of glue to the underside of the tip, wait ten seconds and adhere it to your nail. If you're a nail biter, place it higher on the surface of the nail bed.

4 Apply a few drops of glue to the seam where the tip meets the nail, and let dry.

**Trick of our trade**

Always use non-acetone
remover when removing
polish from nail tips
or wraps.

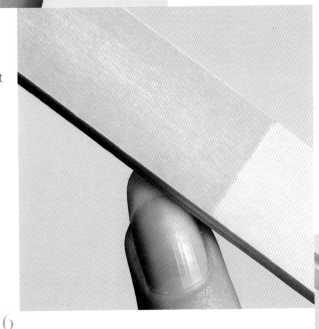

5

To shorten the nail tip to
the desired length, use a
large clipper to cut straight
across the nail.

6

File to any preferred shape,
such as square, oval, or
rounded edges. The most
natural-looking shape is
square with rounded edges.

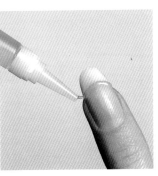

7

Apply more glue to the surface where the seam of the
tip meets with the natural
nail.

8

Let dry, buff, and repeat
until perfectly smooth.

Steps 7 and 8 need not
apply if you're adding a
basic nail wrap or a
sculptured acrylic to the
surface for extra strength.

75

Whether it's a traditional platinum diamond engagement ring, a trendy silver thumb ring, or a sophisticated yellow gold ring filled with gems, adorning hands with jewelry says volumes about you. An accessory to experiment and have fun with, rings—like nail polish—are just another form of self expression. Remember to always take into consideration the design, length, and color of your nails when deciding which rings to wear. For example, if your nails are painted a light, sheer, or solid color, feel free to have fun with big, colorful rings. If your nails are busy with decals, designs, or a bright color, keep the ring selection simple.

*Fun, flowered rings made from lucite are the perfect accessory for clean, beautifully shaped nail extensions. Dramatic-length nail extensions don't always suit sports-minded lifestyles.*

*Our polish pick: natural French manicure.*

# Nail Extensions

A sculptured nail is a fake nail that lays on top of real nails. Made from acrylic powder and bonding liquid (a derivative of a dental acrylic used for artificial teeth), sculptured nails not only add length to your nails, they are also stronger than natural nails.

There are two fundamental reasons to use sculptured nails. The first is for protection. The sculptured nail coats already existing long nails as a protective layer. The second is for strengthening, particularly when used in conjunction with acetate tips.

To achieve a professional-looking set of sculptured nails, you need dexterity in both hands. Before attempting to create your own sculptured nails, observe the entire process in a salon. For sanitary reasons, it's a good idea to bring your own instruments. Be sure to go to a reputable salon – one that sanitizes its tools and is well ventilated. If the fumes overwhelm you when you open the door, find another salon.

A sculptured-nail kit contains a bottle of bonding liquid, a pot of acrylic powder, and a brush. It is imperative that you practice working with the materials due to the fact that the mixture dries very quickly. Soon after you apply the mixture to your nail, it hardens. If you don't know exactly how to manipulate the combination of powder and liquid, it will form bumps on your nails which are extremely difficult to file smooth.

To practice, put a piece of aluminum foil on your table. Dip the brush in the liquid, then take the powder and work with the mixture on the foil. This will help you become familiar with its consistency, i.e., gauge exactly how much you will need on the brush, how to move it around, and how quickly it will dry. As soon as the wet brush touches the powder, a wet ball forms. Work with this ball to create the actual nail. After you feel comfortable with the texture, lay the wet ball on top of your nail and shape it to cover the entire nail.

## How To:  Sculptured Acrylic Nails

**Trick of our trade**

It's worth buying a good sable nail brush for sculptured nails. It will cost approximately eight to twelve dollars, but is well worth the investment.

1
Before you begin, make sure the room you are working in is well ventilated. For your work station, use a towel as a base with layers of paper towels on top.

2
Sanitize your nail by applying a cotton ball moist with alcohol over the entire surface of the nail.

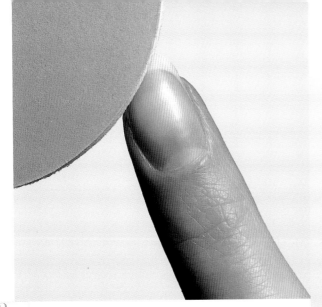

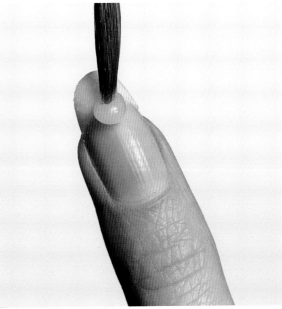

**3**

When the nail is dry, gently rough up the surface of your nail with a buffing disc.

**4**

Keep an open bottle of nail polish remover handy because you will be cleaning off your brush constantly.

**5**

With the acetate tip firmly in place, shortened, and shaped, dip the sable brush in the liquid, wiping off the excess on the sides of the bottle so there isn't too much liquid on the brush.

**6**

Dip the wet brush in the powder pot. A small ball should form on top of the brush.

**7**

Place the ball in the middle of the nail and smooth the cuticle edge first. Be extremely careful not to touch the cuticle. Repeat the process until the entire nail is covered.

**8**

Try to get the sculptured nail as smooth as possible by working the brush around the combined liquid and powder.

**9**

Rinse the brush thoroughly in nail polish remover. Dry on paper towels and repeat until all ten nails are done.

**10**

Tap each sculptured nail with another nail – if it feels hard to the touch, the nail is dry.

**11**

Next, smooth surface bumps with a rough emery board. Then use a buffing disc for a smooth finish.

# Maintenance

Serious maintenance is a must with any artificial nail. If not cared for properly, mold or fungus can appear. A common situation associated with artificial nails is lifting (when the artificial nail begins to lift away from the real nail). As the sculptured nails grow out, there will be a space by the cuticle. Lifting can occur after one month, or sometimes after one week. As soon as it occurs, use a nail nipper to lift the product away or file it off. Sanitize the nail with alcohol and fill it in with small amounts of acrylic. Let it dry, then buff and smooth.

When wearing sculptured nails, avoid direct contact with oils and creams, for they can cause the nail to lift. Be sure to dry nails thoroughly after washing and bathing to prevent moisture from getting under the fake nail.

# Stunning Special Effects

Now that you have created long, beautifully shaped nails, let's add some magic. Sometimes a "special" manicure is called for: a romantic date, graduation, or a festive holiday celebration. Whatever the occasion, choose a look that makes you happy. Following are a few fun ideas.

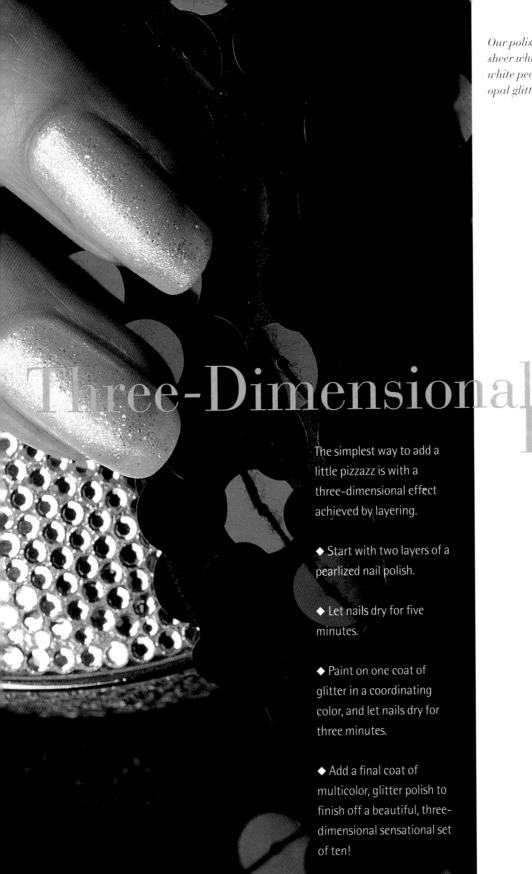

*Our polish pick: one coat of sheer white, one coat of white pearl, and one coat of opal glitter.*

# Three-Dimensional Diva

The simplest way to add a little pizzazz is with a three-dimensional effect achieved by layering.

◆ Start with two layers of a pearlized nail polish.

◆ Let nails dry for five minutes.

◆ Paint on one coat of glitter in a coordinating color, and let nails dry for three minutes.

◆ Add a final coat of multicolor, glitter polish to finish off a beautiful, three-dimensional sensational set of ten!

# Luxurious Nail Gems

Rhinestones, pearls, and crystals need not only adorn necks, wrists, and ears. In fact, they can be purchased in any beauty supply store. These adornments make a wonderful addition to one fingernail, or all ten.

## All that Glitters isn't Always Gold

Glitter dust on nails makes for a fun, retro look. Sold in a cellophane bag, glitter dust should be poured onto a folded piece of paper. It will make an easy applicator.

◆ While your nail polish is still wet, sprinkle glitter on your nails into any design you like. (Make sure to sprinkle it over a sink to avoid a mess.)

◆ When finished, add two coats of clear polish to set it in place.

*Our polish pick: two coats of burgundy creme with two coats of multi-gold glitter.*

**Trick of our trade**

Try using other tools instead of your nails to do busy hand work (i.e., dialing the phone with a pen/pencil; cotton gloves for long extended computer use; rubber gloves for housework).

◆ Pour the gems onto a white piece of paper.

◆ While your nail polish is still damp (not wet) slightly moisten an orangewood stick in water and place gently on a rhinestone or a pearl. The gem should loosely adhere to it. If it doesn't, the stick is too wet.

◆ Once you get it attached, place the gem carefully anywhere on the nail creating a design, or just free form. Let it set for a minute.

◆ Add two coats of clear polish to keep the gem intact.

*Our polish pick (from left to right): two coats of light blue opal with pearl rhinestones, two coats of sea grass shimmer with black rhinestones, two coats of light purple opal with diamond rhinestones.*

# The Joy of Stripes

Striping is another fun and interesting way to spice up a traditional manicure. Sold on a thin roll with an adhesive backing, stripes are fragile to handle, but easy to apply.

◆ Paint your nails with a creme or pearlized formulation. Let them dry at least fifteen to twenty minutes.

◆ Now, unroll the tape to approximately the width of your nail and place a stripe wherever you like. You can use a criss-cross, diagonal, or chevron design, multi-colored stripes, or any other style that you choose.

◆ Take an emery board and file off the excess that extends past the nail tip.

◆ Now that you've mastered this technique, add on some rhinestones or pearls. Get creative by incorporating more than one decorative technique.

*Our polish pick (from left to right): two coats of yellow opal with black-and-white zig zag, two coats of orange opal with gold stripe, three coats of white opal with metallic blue stripes.*

# Darling Decals

Decals come in all shapes and sizes, from florals to geometric designs. They are rather inexpensive. Decals can be used on a clear natural nail or on polished nails. They come in a package affixed to a firm piece of paper and are simple to apply.

*Our polish pick: two coats of lime green pearl with gold butterfly jewelry.*

◆ First, cut out the design you want to use and moisten it with water.

◆ Wait about thirty to sixty seconds, then gently slide it directly onto your nail and press lightly. If there is a bubble, press gently to flatten.

◆ Add two coats of clear polish to affix the decal firmly in place.

## Gold Jewels for Your Nails

Another way to create a unique look is with gold-plated jewelry for nails. They come in all shapes and sizes and look great as an accent on one or two nails. From hearts to butterflies to horoscope signs, they are a fun way to express yourself.

◆ Apply the jewelry just like you would a decal, with one exception: because it is metal, it does not lie flat.

◆ Try bending the metal decal around a pencil in order to create a curve. It will adhere better to the natural bend of the nail.

◆ After it is securely on, use two coats of top coat to hold it in place.

◆ Nail jewelry does tend to come off rather easily. Therefore, stick with gold-plated jewelry instead of expensive 14K.

**Trick of our trade**

Leave air-brushing designs to the professionals! But note – you may be able to find select decals that resemble air brushing designs.

Create Your Own Hand-Painted Designs. Pick a daisy to start.

◆ Apply ridge-filling base coat and one coat of white pearl polish to your nails. Let dry for ten to fifteen minutes.

◆ Dip a narrow-tipped orangewood stick or a pointy toothpick in yellow polish. Make sure that there is no excess polish on the end of the stick.

◆ Using the stick, place five or six dots of polish in a circular pattern on each nail to create petals. Clean the stick in nail polish remover. Make another circular petal, using a blue polish. Place a white dot in the center of the daisy petals.

◆ Dip a fine eyeliner brush in green polish. Wipe off excess polish from the brush. Make small strokes to create two leaves. Let dry ten minutes. End with a clear top coat.

# Press on for Perfection

Press-on nails are pure fun! They can be purchased complete with designs, florals, and solid colors already painted on.

◆ To apply, place one drop of nail glue on the inside of the press-on nail. Wait five seconds.

◆ Place the fake nail onto your fingernail.

◆ Beautiful nails within seconds! Unfortunately, they don't last very long and can pop off in the strangest places when you least expect it. It's a good idea to keep a back-up nail and glue handy in case of a nail emergency.

## Temporary Toenail Art

Now that your fingernails are adorned with beautiful special effects, it's time to treat your toes! Feel free to add decals, stripes, or colored gems to your freshly painted pedicure. Paint each toe a different color or try some glitter polish – just don't do it on the beach. The sun can cause nail polish to bubble and the sand can wreak havoc on a pedicure. Your best bet for experimenting on your feet is at home, the night before you put on your first pair of sandals for the season.

# The Magnificent Art of Mehndi

The newest trend in temporary body art is known as Mehndi and is created with henna. This ancient Middle Eastern art, traditionally used to embellish brides with delicate filigrees, has emerged as an important and chic beauty statement. The beautiful designs have been seen on the hands and feet of many celebrities and supermodels alike.

Available in a kit with distinct designs, the dye is easy to make. Use the ready-made stencil art or create your own designs. It might be wise to experiment with a brown eyeliner when first drawing the design. When you gain confidence, follow directions with the real thing – henna.

◆ Combine lemon juice, oil, sugar, and the dark powder (henna) with boiling water. Let paint mixture stand for fifteen minutes.

◆ Stir for five minutes. Be sure to get rid of all lumps.

◆ Fill the cone (supplied in the kit) with the paint and tape the top shut.

◆ Let the paint sit in the cone for two hours.

◆ Clean the area of the body you intend to paint with oil and lemon juice.

◆ Using a pin, puncture the top of the cone.

◆ Through the tip of the cone, squirt the paint out to create your design.

Let the paint dry for two to six hours depending on how dark you want the design. Scrape off any excess paint with an orangewood stick. Don't wash the area with soap for the first twenty-four hours. Typically, the design should last approximately two weeks depending on how well it takes when it was first applied.

# Nail *and* Hand Care
# Glossary

Now that you're something of an expert on hand and nail care, we thought it would be helpful for you to have definitions of the essentials. Use this chapter as a reference guide whenever you need a quick refresher. It will certainly assist you in determining exactly what you need to properly care for your nails. In fact, make a copy of this glossary and bring it with you the next time you shop the aisles of your favorite beauty supply store. Trust us, it will help you make wise buying decisions based on your individual needs.

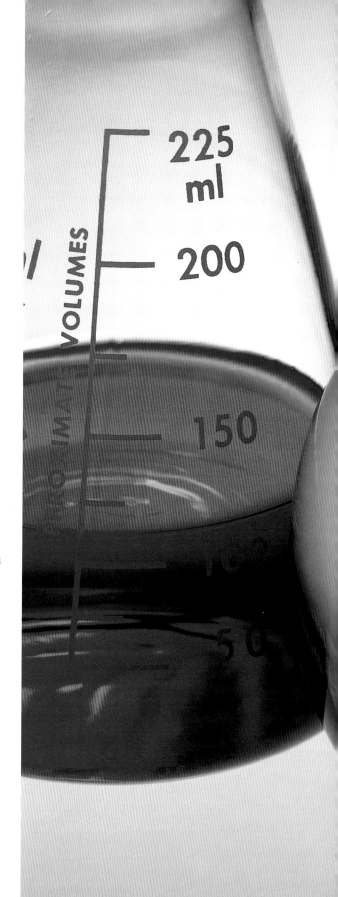

**Acetate Nail Tips** – pre-trimmed artificial nails that can be worn alone or with wraps. They come in many sizes, including oval, square, extra-long, modern oval, ultra-curve, extra-curve, long extra-curve, colored tips, and French tips.

**Acetic Acid** – 5 percent acetic acid is the same as white vinegar.

**Acrylic Sculpture Powder** – helps create a very hard nail by adding strength and reducing cracks and breaks. Can either be used with acrylic sculptured liquid and brush, or with nail glue to repair broken nails.

**Base Coat** – clear nail polish that helps colored nail polish adhere to the nail more effectively. Provides an adhesive bond between the nail surface and the colored polish.

**Buffing Block** – coarse-grade sandpaper block used primarily for shaping and smoothing sculptured nails.

**Buffing Disc** – fine-grade sandpaper disc with a thin cushion in the center. Used to smooth off rough nail edges or to buff the surface of the nail.

**Buffing Paste** – cream used with chamois buffer to create a shine on natural nails.

**Burows Solution** – aluminum acetate, also known as a topical astringent. Available in liquid form.

**Chamois Buffer** – soft piece of leather used on natural nails to achieve a smooth, shiny surface.

**Cuticle Cream Groomer** – stick that softens, conditions, and moistens hard, dry cuticles. Can also be used to gently push back cuticles.

**Cuticle Nipper** – metal plier-like instrument used to snip hangnails and torn cuticles.

**Cuticle Remover** – exfoliates the dry, rough, outer

# Nail *and* Hand Care Glossary

layer of the cuticle. A remover with vitamin E and/or aloe will allow a healthier cuticle to grow.

**Cuticle Softener** – softens the cuticle area to aid in pushing cuticles back.

**Emery Board** – sandpaper-like texture that comes in many grades of roughness. Finer grades are recommended – they're easier on the nails.

**Foot Scraper** – used to scrape rough, dry skin from the bottom of the foot. Only use when skin on the foot is wet.

**Gel Overlay** – a coat of clear gel that provides maximum durability to the nail. Can be used on natural nails or tips for extra protection.

**Glue** – offers adhesion. Available in brush form as well as the traditional tube.

**Liquid Fiber Wrap** – base coat that contains fibers to strengthen weak, peeling nails.

**Metal Nail File** – this type of file is much too abrasive for filing nails. It can, however, be used to clean underneath nails.

**Nail Brush** – used to clean over and under nails soaked in warm water. Soft bristles are recommended for a gentler scrub.

**Nail Buffer** – chamois fabric used to buff nails to create a smooth and shiny surface.

**Nail Clippers** – used for trimming fingernails.

**Nail Enamel Corrector** – polish remover pen used to touch up mistakes around cuticles and nail edges resulting from color application.

**Nail File** – a sandpaper-like texture, used for shaping nails. A soft grain is recommended. Abrasive files tend to disrupt healthy nail growth.

**Nail Filler** – acrylic powder that is sprinkled over the

# Nail *and* Hand Care Glossary

entire nail for joining a tip to a natural nail. Also for emergency repair. Always use with nail glue.

**Nail Hardener** – clear nail polish that strengthens and protects nails. Can also be used to bond and seal wraps and tips.

**Nail Polish Remover** – use regular acetone formula with moisture for natural nails; use non-acetone for artificial nails.

**Nail Polish Remover Dip Jar** – a jar filled with remover and a sponge. Remove polish by rubbing nails against the sponge. It is not recommended for dark colored polishes, as they can rub off onto hands and nails.

**Nail Primer** – clear form of polish that removes moisture, oil, and shine from the natural nail. Provides maximum strength between natural nails and acrylic. Can also be used before glue application to prepare nails for easier glue adhesion.

**Nail Strengthener** – clear nail polish used to strengthen weak, brittle nails by sealing in moisture. Can be used as a base coat or alone. Some nail strengthening formulas contain nylon for the ultimate in nail-hardening.

**Nail Tip Clipper** – instrument with custom-shaped blade used to cut artificial nail tips and acrylic nails without splitting or cracking the nail.

**Nail Whitener** – white pencil for heightening the whiteness of nail tips. Used underneath the tip of the nail.

**Nourishing Gel Capsules** – liquid capsules containing alpha hydroxy acid which gently exfoliate the skin around nails and cuticles.

**Orangewood Stick** – thin wood stick used to push back cuticles and clean underneath nails.

**Pumice Stick** – used to push back and smooth out

# Nail *and* Hand Care Glossary

rough cuticles and bumps, such as a callus on your writing finger.

**Pumice Stone** – used on dry, rough feet to smooth away dead skin.

**Ridge Filler** – opaque base coat that fills the ridges of the nail for a smooth surface. Used in preparation for applying colored nail polish.

**Sculptured Nails** – fake nails made from acrylic powder and bonding liquid that add length to natural nails, and/or strengthen nails.

**Silk Wraps** – thin fabric used to repair or reinforce nail strength.

**Smoothing Block** – a fine-grit, cushioned emery block that is used to curve and contour the shape of a nail, nail tip, wrap, or acrylic nail.

**Toe Spacer** – sponge separator that fits in between toes to prevent them from touching one another when polish is applied.

**Toenail Clippers** – large metal clippers used for trimming toenails and artificial nails only.

**Top Coat** – clear nail polish used after color is applied. It seals in the color polish for longer wear and protects the nail polish from chipping and dulling.

**Water Decal** – a temporary, tattoo-like design applied to polished nails.

**White Tip Guides** – used as an aid to create a French manicure. The adhesive stickers are placed below the white of the nail. White polish is then painted over the guide.

# Acknowledgments

This book flew out of nowhere, essentially overnight, but not without the help of our own incredible dream team who brought their superb expertise to the project:

For our publisher, Charles Miers, and senior editor, Sandy Gilbert, who believed in the great idea of a hand and nail care book—we thank you a thousand times; Stephanie Seymour, whose gifts, friendship, and practical advice helped launch this book; Valerie DeSoto, who donated inspiration and ideas; Dana Epstein, our writer, who gave a voice to our thoughts and ideas; our wonderful graphic designer, Debra Drodvillo, who magically created a finished product from all of our loose ends; Joe Neil, our photographer, who created beautiful images beyond our greatest expectations; and his wife, Paula, for putting up with late nights and early mornings; Joe's assistant, Tony Fuori, who sustained our lunacy on set; and Michelle Brahin, who graciously gave her lips, feet, and time to our cause.

Many thanks to Rob Kapnek and Monique Burgess for introducing us to Joe a long time ago; Mark Maltais, who began this design project and got us off to a great jump-start; and Alice Martell, for her counsel and guidance throughout this project.

For our generous friends in the jewelry industry: Ellen Soto, Marvella, and Trifari of the Monet Group, Inc., whose amazing jewelry graces our pages; SKF International for some spectacular cuffs (skfnet@aol.com); Wendy Tabb NYC who gave us her exquisite jewelry (tabbnyc@girlshop.com!); Ted Frankel at Uncle Fun, Chicago, for his playful flowered rings (unclfun@aol.com); and Lynn Freidus for her quick connections.

Special thanks to Kim Rizzardi at Kiss Products and Broadway who quickly responded to our design needs; Lisa's agents, Carmen Marrufo and Marge Tate at TRH—the most incredible agents in the world; Elisa's agent, Jenny Lister, not only a dedicated agent but a wonderful friend who made this vision a reality; Belina who made sense of Elisa's hectic schedule; everyone at Agora Cosmetics; and François Nars, whose generosity added color and brightness to our pages .

We are very grateful to five individuals who offered expertise in their respective fields: Dr. Fusco, a dermatologist at the Wexler Group, New York City, contributed key information pertaining to nail and skin problems and solutions. Charlene Greco DePalma, a nutritionist in Westchester, NY, helped us realize the crucial role diet and vitamins play in achieving healthy skin and nails. David Larkin, a massage therapist in Westchester, NY, taught us what a good hand massage is all about. Uncle Ignatius Paolilla shared his knowledge and experience in reflexology. Selma Gilbert, a nutritionist, fine-tuned and confirmed our thoughts and questions.

This book belongs to all of us.